RORKE'S DRIFT DIARY

RORKE'S DRIFT DIARY

An account of the Battles of Isandhlwana and
Rorke's Drift, Zululand 22nd January 1879

William Penn Symons

UNIFORM

First published in 1879

Published by Uniform in 2018
an imprint of Unicorn Publishing Group

Unicorn Publishing Group
101 Wardour Street
London W1F 0UG

www.unicornpublishing.org

A catalogue record for this book is
available from the British Library

ISBN 978-1-91160-424-2

Printed and bound in Great Britain by
ImprintDigital.com
Cover design Unicorn Publishing Group

Typeset by Graham Hales

Contents

The following diary has been faithfully reproduced from an original manuscript, typed up from handwritten notes not long after the events portrayed. As such there may be discrepancies in spellings when compared to other material on this subject matter. The publishers have made minor alterations where known but otherwise kept spellings and text in keeping with the source document. This has the additional benefit of continuity for anyone who may wish to reference the original, housed in the Victoria Cross Trust Museum.

Introduction

Neil Thornton

ON 11 January 1879, Lord Chelmsford and the British central column consisting of the 1st and 2nd Battalions of the 24th (2nd Warwickshire) Regiment, together with a number of other units, crossed the Natal border into Zululand. The aim – to topple the Zulu kingdom – was expected to be achieved without exertion. However, just eleven days later, on the 22nd, a large portion of the column, camped under the watchful gaze of the iSandlwana mountain, came under attack by an estimated 20,000 warriors of King Cetshwayo's Zulu Army. The attack resulted in the complete annihilation of the camp, with almost every man of the 24th Foot falling on the field of battle. That morning, prior to the attack on the camp, and acting on information that the

Zulus had been spotted in great numbers ten miles distant, Lord Chelmsford, with approximately half of his available force had departed from iSandlwana, enthusiastically advancing deeper into Zululand in pursuit of his enemy.

The sighting would prove to be something of a red herring and when the column returned to iSandlwana they found a scene of carnage and destruction awaiting them. The camp had fallen, and the bodies of their comrades, ritually mutilated and disembowelled, were strewn across the battlefield.

Chelmsford's remaining force spent a weary night amongst these horrors. Before first light they set off towards Rorke's Drift, fully expecting a repeat of the sight that had awaited them at iSandlwana, but at the same time hoping against hope that a large body of survivors had fought their way out and succeeded in reaching the mission station. In the latter respect their hopes were soon dashed, but against all odds it was discovered that the men stationed at the post – chiefly 'B' Company, 2/24th, had in fact held the place after fighting off multiple sustained and determined attacks against their hastily erected defensive barricades by an enemy far superior in number.

Amongst those men returning with Lord Chelmsford was William Penn Symons (sometimes written as Symonds), a company commander in the 2/24th. Symons and the other members of the column remained cooped up at the drift for a lengthy period after that fateful day.

During this period Symons spoke with those who had taken part in the defence, recording what had happened and noting their experiences. He would also write of, and analyse, the iSandlwana disaster. This publication is the result of his efforts.

It would be impertinent to introduce this account without providing some detail of the man responsible for it. William Penn Symons was a career soldier, fiercely loyal to his regiment and, in the words of one contemporary, 'as brave as a lion [and] a man who had but two ideals, one duty, and the other that of doing his duty in all circumstances in the spirit of a high-minded, chivalrous gentleman.'[1] Later in his career Symons would command the regiment's 2nd Battalion, and his passion for documenting events saw him acknowledged as a leading contributor to the Regiment history.[2]

Born on 17 July 1843 in Saltash, Cornwall, Symons joined the 24th Regiment as an Ensign in March 1863, aged nineteen. He was promoted to lieutenant in 1866 and to captain shortly before the Anglo-Zulu War, in 1878.

In the years following the Zulu War, Symons saw extensive service and enjoyed rapid promotion.

By the time of the Second Boer War in 1899, he was commanding a division. On 20 October 1899, during the opening stages of the conflict he issued orders for his force to attack the Boers on Talana Hill but the attack stalled under heavy fire before a stretch of open ground in front of the hill. Symons then rode to the forefront, dismounted, and advanced into the open to get the attack moving again.

Ultimately the hill would be taken but Symons, after returning to his horse and being assisted by his aide in remounting it, rode back from the front line. Only then did he let it be known that he had been mortally wounded by a gunshot to his stomach. Symons died three days later. His final words, spoken to a medical officer, were: 'Tell everyone I died facing the enemy; tell everyone I died facing the enemy!'[3]

Symons, who was fifty-six years old, was buried in Dundee near to where he died.[4] Ironically, despite serving all over the world, his final resting place is just twenty miles from Rorke's Drift – the root of this publication.

This account by Symons, is reproduced from the leather-bound version in possession of The Victoria Cross Trust, is of vital importance and a welcome addition to the readily available sources which aid our understanding of those two incredible actions that took place on 22/23 January 1879, the outcomes of which were in stark contrast to one another. Whilst the account is a valuable research source in its own right, it also serves as a stand-alone exciting read for those seeking a fast-paced narrative of the battles.

In some respects the views and testimonies documented by Symons may not necessarily always correspond with those given by other sources, both contemporary and those formulated by the modern revisionist. This is typical of the complexities of the Anglo-Zulu War and the many conundrums, theories and counter-theories that surround it are what make this war such a fascinating and captivating subject to study.

This account will hold appeal to researchers, historians and enthusiasts alike, and is a vital cog in our understanding the events, and the thought processes and actions of those who were there.

Symons, and as a result – this publication, also provides us with the first-hand accounts of Privates Williams, Bickley and Wilson of the 1/24th, together with that of Colonel Glyn's interpreter, Mr Brickhill, all of whom survived iSandlwana. These witness testimonies provide crucial detail regarding the events at iSandlwana, an event that saw only a handful of the very limited number of survivors record their experiences.

I commend both The Victoria Cross Trust and Unicorn Publishing Group for bringing this substantial account to the wider audience that it so richly deserves.

Neil Thornton
(September 2017)

An account of the Battle of Isandhlwana

Zululand 22nd January 1879. We crossed the Buffalo River which divides Natal from Zululand at Rorke's Drift on the 11th of January 1879. Our force, the 3rd Column, was under Command of Col. Glyn. 1/24th Regt.

Two other Columns were to advance simultaneously one, from the North from Luneberg; the other from the South, crossing the Tugela River at its mouth, under Col. Pearson 2/3rd Regt.

This has only to do with the 3rd Column to which we belonged.

Lt. Gen. Lord Chelmsford KCB, commanding the forces in S. Africa, and his Staff were with us, and he personally directed the movements of the Column.

The crossing was unopposed and successfully accomplished by the aid of 2 Pontoons and a boat. The river at this point is 80 yards wide and the current rapid. Horses and oxen crossed lower down, 300 yards below at the 'Old Drift' or crossing place. The water was there girth deep, and though several were washed off their legs, all eventually got safely across.

The following is a list of the Troops composing the Column:

1. N. Battery, 5th Bde, R. Artillery under Col. Harness, 5 Officers, 126 NCOs and Men.
2. 5 Companies of the 1/24th Regt. under Capt. W. Degacher, 16 Officers, 375 NCOs and Men.
3. 7 Companies of the 2/24th Regt. under Col. Degacher CB, 23 Officers and 748 NCOs and Men.
4. Natal Mounted Police under Maj. Dartnell, 4 Officers, 128 Troopers.
5. Natal Carbineers (Volunteers) under Capt. Shepstone, 10 Officers, 90 NCOs and Troopers.
6. Buffalo Border Guard.
7. 1st Squadron Mounted Infantry under Maj. Russell 12th Lan, 4 Officers, 107 rank and file.
8. Natal Native Contingent under Comdt. Lonsdale, 63 Officers, 124 NCOs, white men, 2,400 natives.

9. Army Hospital Corps, 11 NCOs and Men.

We pitched our Camp immediately on the river and it was protected by a chain of picquets 1½ miles from the Camp extended in a semicircle with the ends resting on the river.

On the morning of the 12th reports were brought in that the Zulus were chanting their war songs, and herding cattle 4 miles off. Leaving a sufficient force to guard the Camp we moved out at 7 am. At 8.15 a.m., Maj. Black, who was in temporary Command of Lonsdale's contingent, commenced firing on the side of a rocky and precipitous hill, locally termed a Krantz, on the Southern side of the Bashee Valley.

Companies of the 2/24th Regt. and 400 of the native levies under Col. Degacher CB worked round the 'Krantz' so as to take the enemy in the left flank. Maj. Black, however, soon drove them out of the caves to which they had retired, killing 11. He lost two of the Contingent dead (1 Officer, 1 NCO) and 12 native wounded. He himself was struck in the back by a fragment of rock, rolled down by Zulus from above, but was not seriously injured.

An hour afterwards we the main body advanced to attack Sirayo's Kraal. It was this chief's son who had carried off and murdered 2 refugee Zulu women from our territory, one of the chief causes of complaint against Cetewayo the King, as he would give no satisfaction for the outrage. To our disappointment the Kraal was deserted. It was picturesquely situated in an angle of the hills, 200 ft above the level of the Valley and well watered. It consisted of 57 huts built round a circular cattle pen. We looted and then burnt the huts.

The chief prize was a large bed of onions with which the men filled their haversacks, 3 old women and one little girl were found in a cave above the Kraal. They said that the men, women and cattle had all left on the previous day for the Kings Kraal (Ulundi).

We captured 700 head of cattle in the Valley on the way back. On the hills above the Krantzes the mounted Infantry and Police did good work. They came on about 100 of the enemy and killed 16, amongst them one of Sirayo's sons, and this without any loss to themselves.

On the 14th, 4 Companies of the 2/24th Regt, 100 native Pioneers and the 2/3rd N.N.C., all under Command of Maj. Dunbar 2/24th Regt., were pushed on about 5 miles to the Bashee river for the purpose of road making.

On the 18th a report came in that 3 Impis (Zulu for Army or Regiment) had left the Kings Kraal to attack us. Up to the 20th January preparations were continued for an advance; wagons and stores were got across the river and a road made through the Bashee Valley.

We left at daybreak on the morning of this day all in the best of spirits at a move at last, after so many months of preparation and waiting.

The Column extended to a great length, we had 110 wagons each of which was drawn by a span of 16 or 14 oxen. The rear guard took the whole day to accomplish 8 miles, and this over roads that a large body of men had been making for a week.

By the morning of the 21st, all the troops were encamped at the foot of the Isandhlwana Hill. This is a steep rocky eminence, 600 to 700 feet high rising boldly from the surrounding undulating country. In shape it is like a Sphinx (the badge of the 24th Regt.) or Lion, and it is accessible and that with difficulty at one or two points only. The name in the Zulu language signifies the small or ruminating paunch of the ox. The Camp was pitched at the front of the hill facing South East. In front a broad valley, on either side ridges of hills.

The 1/24 Regt. was on the right, the different mounted Corps, next then the Artillery, next the 2/24th Regt. and the N.N.C. on the extreme left; the whole occupying a frontage of about 800 yards. Most of the Wagons were scattered about the ridge on our right rear, preparatory to being sent back to Rorke's Drift for further supplies.

The Generals' Camp was pitched in rear of the centre, close under the scarped face of the hill.

Everyone turned in early that night not dreaming even of what was in store for the morrow. Indeed so far the invasion had been as Autumn manoeuvres in pleasant but hot weather in England. Officers with permission went out alone shooting and prospecting miles from the Camp with no thought of risk or danger.

Towards evening on the 21st of January the General was informed that there was reason to believe that large bodies of the enemy were collecting behind the hills on the left front of the Camp. Col. Glyn suggested that Scouts and patrols should be sent out in the morning to examine into the truth or otherwise of this intelligence. Subsequent reports most unfortunately altered this intention and on this wise: two thirds of the N.N.C. under Comdt. Lonsdale and the main part of the Police and Volunteers under Maj. Dartnell had been sent out at 5 a.m. to scour the hills and Krantzes on the right of the Valley. Maj. Gosset and Capt. Buller, 2 of Lord C's ADCs, accompanied this force and at 3 p.m. Zulus in some numbers were discovered in their front. Maj. Dartnell sent in to report that he had felt the enemy, and he proposed to remain where he was so as to keep them in view and bivouac. Permission was granted and the force rested for the night 10 miles from the Camp.

In a second report, which reached the General at 1 a.m., Maj. Dartnell stated that the enemy were in force on the hilltops in his front; that he proposed attacking them at 6 a.m. and he suggested that 2 Companies of the 24th Regt. should be sent out to his support. On this intelligence and in accordance with the declared intentions of the General to attack the enemy whenever and wherever they could be found, at the first streak of dawn on the 22nd of January 6 Companies of the 2/24th Regt., 4 guns and the Mounted Infantry left Camp to join the Police and Volunteers and make a combined movement against the enemy under the personal direction of the Lt. Gen. Commanding.

At first the 1/24th Regt had been warned to go out, but on account of the 2nd Battalion being the stronger they were ordered to go instead. During the night there had been one or two false alarms amongst the N.N.C. in their advanced bivouac. Some few Companies stood their ground, but the majority regularly stampeded, rushing over, and in one or two cases knocking down their Officers who were in their midst and wounding each other with their assegais.

Their Officers from this time lost all faith in them and there is no doubt that had the Zulus attacked them that night the natives would have bolted, and considering their undefended and isolated position it is improbable that a single white man belonging to the Police Volunteers or N.N.C. could have escaped.

To defend and guard the Camp, 5 Companies of the 1/24th Regt., 2 guns, 62 gunners under Lt. Curling RA, 1 Company of the 2/24th Regt. under Lt. Pope, a few mounted men the remainder of the N.N.C. (about 800) and numerous casuals and idlers were left behind. There were about 850 white soldiers and as many black men – a force that at the time, and acting under the orders given, could not have been considered sufficient to repel any attack that could have been made by savages. It was under Command of Lt. Col. Pulleine, 1/24th Regt. This Officer had lately arrived from Pietermaritzburg, and had taken over the Command of his Battalion. He received written orders from the Officer in Command of the Column 'to keep his men in Camp, to act strictly on the defensive, draw in the Infantry *and* extend the Cavalry picquets', Maj. Clery Staff Officer to Col. Glyn before he left the Camp asked Col. Pulleine if he understood these orders and was answered in the affirmative.

The brunt of an attack would have to be borne by the 1/24th Regiment; and in the British Army it would have been impossible to pick a body of men fitter for such work. The majority of them were old soldiers of ten years' service and over, of grand physique, self-confident, and fresh from the successful campaign in the Old Colony.

To follow our main body first

WE marched 12 miles. We then saw the enemy in scattered bodies of from 10 to 500 dispersing and retreating in front of us in all directions. We followed them. It was hunting a shadow, or worse than a shadow, as men, who well knew the Zulus, their character and tactics, declare that the cattle which had been seen, and the retreating bodies of men, were simply a decoy to entice us away from the Camp.

Be this as it may, the enemy that we went out to look for were marching in a direction parallel to our line of advance behind a range of hills 3 miles only to the left to attack the Camp. It will be asked was there no scouting? It must be answered none.

The Column was now split up into detachments. The Mounted Police and N.N.C. supported by two Companies of the 2/24th Regt. under Maj. Dunbar came across a few of the enemy hiding in caves. They killed 30 and took some prisoners after a slight resistance.

At 9.30 a.m. (time vouched by Capt. Hallam Parr ADC) Maj. Clery received a dispatch from Col. Pulleine saying that 'The Zulus advancing in force from left front of the Camp'. This as noted in the despatch was sent off at 8.05 a.m., Maj. Clery handed it to the General who read it and said 'There is nothing to be done on that'. Just before 10 a.m. there was a halt for Breakfast and the General sent Lt. Milne RA ADC and Capt. Symons 2/24th Regiment with a party of signallers up a high hill, from which the Camp and the Isandhlwana Hill, distance some ten miles could plainly be seen with two powerful telescopes that they took with them. Beyond noticing that some of the oxen seemed to be collected about the wagons, all seemed quiet in Camp, and at that time it was certain that no firing was going on. They saw about two miles off, about 500 of the enemy retreating away from the Camp, and the halted Column round the foot of the Isipesi mountain, Col. Russell and the Mounted Infantry engaged them and drove them further off.

At 10 o'clock a.m., the General sent in Mounted Officers with orders for Col. Pulleine to strike and send out our portion of the Camp and seven days rations to us. Capt. Allen Gardner 14th Hussars took the order and was accompanied by Maj. Stuart Smith RA, Lt. McDowell RE, and a small escort. They reached the Camp about 11.30 a.m., and joined in the fight that then took place.

Col. Pulleine in the absence of Col. Durnford (to be explained later) received the order and sent a despatch in answer to the General which was received by him and was to the effect, 'That he did not think that he would be able to comply with the order just at present as the enemy were showing themselves in great force on our left front, it should be done, however, as soon as possible'. We will letter this despatch 'L'.

Since this was written we have heard that Lord. C. says that he never received this despatch. We know that it was sent off by Col. Pulleine and it was generally understood by those in the reconnoitring Column that some such despatch was received. It was passed round that there would be a delay in the arrival of our tents and that we might have to bivouac for the night without them or food.

At 10.30 o'clock that morning Comdt. Browne N.N.C. was ordered to take his men back to Camp. They had been out the previous day and night without food *and* were famished. 5 or 6 miles from Camp he perceived large bodies of Zulus on his right moving towards the Camp. He sent a report in writing of this to the General about noon. On receiving it the General was asked by his Military Secretary Col. Crealock in the hearing of several Officers if he would not alter his plans. He said, 'No, not at all.'

A little further on Comdt. Browne heard and saw firing on the left of the Camp, and at the same time three separate strings of Zulus, in all estimated by him at 3,000 men, marching from his right to his left, stopping his advance and cutting him off from the Camp.

There seems every probability that these are the men that we shall hear of again at Rorke's Drift.

Not being able to advance, Comdt. Browne took up a good position and waited. He sent another emphatic despatch by an Officer with a mounted man of the N.N.C to the General. It ran 'For God's sake send every man back to Camp, it is surrounded and will be taken unless helped at once'. The bearer communicated its purport to Capt. Church 2/24 Regiment, who, seeing two men galloping towards him over the plain, borrowed a trumpeter's horse from Col. Harness RA and rode to meet them.

Having told Capt. Church they galloped on and he reported to Col. Harness. This Officer with his 4 guns and 2 Companies of the 2/24th as escort had been sent round to the intended new Camping ground, whilst the Infantry and Mounted Troops moved in detached bodies by more circuitous routes over the hills.

Col. Harness with the concurrence of Maj. Black D.A.A.M.G., though strongly advised by Maj. Gossett ADC to obey orders and not to do so, started his party at once for the Isandhlwana Camp. This was soon after 1 p.m. They had gone about two miles and a half when they were stopped by Maj. Gossett, who had ridden back and returned from the General, with orders to retrace their steps. As they were returning they met the General and his Staff proceeding at a walk towards the Camp.

Comdt. Lonsdale now met the General and confirmed the rumours that up to this time had in no way been believed. His story was: anxious that his camp should be struck properly, and tired out and faint with hunger *and* craving for food *and* rest he had ridden back in a sort of listless trance by himself, and seeing men in red coats moving about in Camp, and all being quiet, had not noticed anything wrong but rode right on across the 'Donga' into Camp. Suddenly seeing a Zulu covered with blood come out of a tent and scowl at him, it flashed on him that the Zulus dressed in our soldiers' coats were in possession. At first his pony 'Dot', also dead beat, would not turn or move away from the direction of his picket rope, but being persuaded the Commandant got him round and galloped for his life, and regaining the road in spite of the enemy closing in on him and trying to cut off his retreat, charged down it and escaped without being touched by a bullet or assegai, numbers of which were aimed at him.

This occurred at 1.45 p.m. (about).

In the meantime the component parts of the main body had collected on the Camping ground near the Mangeni Valley 12 miles from Isandhlwana and waiting for the arrival of the camp equipage had 'Fallen out' and most of the men were asleep. At five minutes past four Maj. Gossett rode back with orders for us to return whence we had come in the morning at our best pace. A whisper ran round that the Camp had been taken and sacked. No one credited it. The men had had a long day's march in the hot sun. They stepped out bravely, however, and at ten minutes after six had covered miles half the distance.

Here we met the General who in a few stirring words told us that the enemy had taken the Camp. He addressed the 2/24th Regt. saying: '24th whilst we have been out yonder the enemy has outflanked us and taken our Camp, they are probably holding it now; at any cost we must take it back tonight and cut our way back to Rorke's Drift tomorrow. This means fighting but I know that I can rely upon you? The men answered with a cheer, "All right Sir".'

As the General turned away he said, 'That's all right.'

The Column now advanced at a great pace. As we marched on we could see on the skyline on our right parties of the enemy retiring over the Tugutu hills (*sic*) with their spoil from the Camp and driving herds of cattle 'our trek oxen' and some wagons with them.

Darkness quickly came on. Half a mile from Camp we halted and deployed into line.

Maj. Black with the left Companies of the 2/24th and half the N.N.C. first advanced with orders to take and occupy the stony Kopje (small hill) to the left of the nek.

A few shells were now fired from the guns as feelers to force the enemy if present to unmask. There was no response. All was still as death. Then, in total darkness, in line, the 4 guns in the centre, the remainder with bayonets fixed advanced on the hill. It was a most trying time for the young soldiers, indeed for all. Every instant we expected to be attacked. As we neared the Camp we stumbled constantly, horror upon horror, over the naked, gashed and ghastly bodies of our late comrades. We gained the ridge or nek at 8.15 p.m.; the Isandhlwana hill close on our right flank, Maj. Black and his force on the Kopje on our left. Here we spent a terrible night. We formed an oblong of guns and horses in the centre and lay or sat down in the ranks. It was bitterly cold. The mutilated dead were around us and in our midst. No one slept.

During the night there were several false alarms from the N.N.C. who hung like an incubus on our right; they were thoroughly panic stricken, and had now shown themselves completely untrustworthy. Their Officers and NCOs could scarcely keep them from rushing in upon us, and they from time to time let off their guns in the air without aim or object.

The white soldiers kept quite steady, nothing could be more quiet or staunch than their behaviour.

Between 10 p.m. and midnight we heard firing towards Rorke's Drift and on the hills all round we could see the enemy's beacon fires burning.

At the first sign of the anxiously looked for daybreak we formed column of march and left for Rorke's Drift.

The General and his Staff fully believed that we had our Impi in our rear and another in front through which we should have to cut our way. We had no provisions and only 70 rounds of ammunition per man. They therefore very wisely judged that it would be wrong to sicken and dispirit the men by a sight of the stricken Camp by daylight. Some of the Officers applied for leave to go and have a short search for the Colours that we feared might have been lost, and all would have had liked to have time to go and bury the dead, and afterwards search for letters and papers more valuable than other lost possessions. But permission could not be granted and no one left the Column or remained behind.

At this time we never imagined for an instant that the whole of the force left to guard the Camp had been well nigh exterminated.

We hoped and expected to find the greater part of it at Rorke's Drift.

We arrived there on the Natal side at 8.30 a.m. without encountering any of the enemy, though two large bodies made their appearance on our left rear without, however, coming near enough to enable us to fire a shot. Fortunately, the Pontoons had been left untouched and we crossed easily.

Battle of Rorke's Drift

ONE mile from the Buffalo River Lt. Bromhead with his Company (Letter 'B') had been left to guard Commissariat Stores and the lines of communication. The Company numbered 90 men and besides these there were 40 casuals, 35 of whom were patients in hospital.

Lt. Chard RE was the senior Officer present and Lt. Bromhead and his Company worked and acted under his able superintendence and orders.

The post had been desperately attacked by great numbers of the enemy from 4 p.m., on the preceding afternoon till daylight.

Brevet. Maj. Spalding DAQM had ridden from Rorke's Drift to Helpmakaar in the morning to hurry down the two Companies of the 1/24th Regt, left behind there to assist in protecting the Ponts and Stores. They got to the bottom of the

Biggarsberg range of hills 5 miles from Rorke's Drift at dusk, and the advanced party, seeing the Hospital in flames halted, and it was decided to return to Helpmakaar.

They arrived there at 12.30 a.m., and joined in forming a laagar that was then being made. Had Helpmakaar been attacked during their absence, only 37 rifles counting escaped fugitives could have been mustered for a defence.

At 3 p.m., on the 22nd January, Lt. Bromhead received the startling news from two fugitives that the Generals' Camp was taken, and that the Zulus were on the way to attack his post. These men lost no time in continuing their journey, and it is fortunate for them that Lt. Bromhead was unable to recognise them afterwards. Half an hour afterwards the intelligence was confirmed by a hastily written note from Capt. Allen Gardner 14th Hussars. It will be remembered that this Officer was one of those sent in by Lord Chelmsford with orders to remove a portion of the Camp.

He got into Camp, acted as Staff Officer to Col. Pulleine, stayed till the last moment and then escaped across the river. After going a little way he overtook Capt. Essex 75th Regt. and Lt. Cochrane 32nd Regt. who had also escaped from Isandhlwana. These two Officers now in safety had stopped to consult on the best thing to do. Believing that the road to Rorke's Drift was blocked to themselves by Zulus, and ignorant of the path, they decided to send a mounted native with a note, Capt. Gardner, the only possessor of a pencil and paper, wrote the message at Capt. Essex's dictation, and the three Officers rode on together to Helpmakaar, the next post in the line of communications.

Capt. Essex and Lt. Cochrane remained there but Capt. Gardner rode on at once to Dundee without dismounting, and his own horse being by this time thoroughly done up, he gave a Dutchman £20 to ride to Utrecht, when after warning that place, he was to go on to Col. Wood's Camp and apprise him. Capt. Gardner, however, obtained a fresh horse next morning and riding by a shorter route arrived at Utrecht just at the same time as the Dutchman, and having sent on a message to Col. Wood by an Artillery man called Cook, he rode back to Rorke's Drift.

The above warning gave the Officer at Rorke's Drift a short hour for preparation. It was badly needed as nothing had been done to prepare the place for defence; the arrangements for so doing having been put off 'by order' until the arrival of the expected reliefs of the Royal Engineers and 4th Regt. The tents of the Company were pitched outside a farmhouse or rather houses, as there were two; one was used as a store, the other as a base Hospital and they were 40 yards apart. At this time Lt. Chard was engaged at the Ponts and receiving the same intelligence of the disaster and intended attack from another fugitive, moved the Ponts in the middle of the stream and made the best of his way back to where Lt. Bromhead and Actg. Commissariat Officer Dalton were doing their utmost to render the place defensible.

The tents were struck and the houses loopholed and occupied. They then managed to pile a few biscuit boxes and mealie sacks as a sort of parapet towards the garden on one side, and along the other facing the hill, which completely commanded the houses and enclosures. They drew up three wagons and filled up the gaps with more boxes and sacks of grain. These 'lines' connected the two houses and formed what we will call 'the yard'. It was a broken and imperfect barricade at the best; on the garden side nowhere more than 3 ft high towards the hill they raised it in places to 4 and 4½ ft high. The Advanced Guard of the Zulus first appeared about 4.30 p.m. It came round the South corner of the hill in a body 500 to 600 strong, and led by a Chief riding a grey mare. They halted a moment, and then advanced quietly but quickly at a run taking advantage of every bit of cover. It seemed as though they had expected to surprise the Camp. Our men opened fire at 500 yds. The first man to fall was the mounted Chief. He was shot by Pte. Dunbar and fell headlong. Numbers of them fell at once. As soon as the enemy felt the fire they broke and the greater part scattered to their left and occupied the garden and orchard where there was plenty of cover. A few got up close to the houses and lay behind the field ovens and kitchens, that were there built, but these were quickly shot. A few only of these men had guns or rifles. In a continuous stream more of them came on, occupied the hill and gradually encircled the two houses, most of the men who had guns were stationed on the hill, and they kept up a rapid fire on the yard. It caught our men in reverse as they manned the garden side, and five men were thus shot dead. As the evening set in, the dusky foe crept nearer and nearer. Under the cover of the bushes and long grass they were able to get within 5 yds of the Hospital without being seen. From this point in parties of 15 to 20 they repeatedly attacked the corners of the Hospital. They made these attacks in the most deliberate manner. As in their dancing they stalked out of their concealment, pranced up with a high stepping action, and caring nothing for the slaughter, endeavoured to get over the barricade and into the end room of the Hospital. Many times (seven or eight at least) Lt. Bromhead collected a few men together and drove them off with a bayonet charge. On being repulsed they would retire to better cover, and in a sort of chorus shout beat their shields with their assegais. Our men cheered in response and let them have it. How deliberate and hitting the fire was may be gathered from the following incidents.

Pte. Joseph. Williams, a young Welshman of under two years' service, had a small window from the far end of the Hospital to shoot from. Next morning 14 dead warriors were found dead outside the window and many more down his line of fire. As soon as his ammunition was all expended he and the other men in the room with him defended the door with their bayonets till it was broken and forced open.

Poor fellow he was seized by the arms and hands, dragged out and assegaied and mutilated before the eyes of his comrades. Another instance, Pte. Dunbar, the same man who had shot the Chief on horseback, was posted to watch the hill. As the Zulus streamed round the foot from the right, this man of even less service than the other, got the right distance and shot eight of them in as many consecutive shots. Lt. Chard was standing by him as he did it.

At last by sheer weight of numbers they burst in the doors of the Hospital and effected a lodgement. 28 of the patients were got out in time. Most of them were pushed or pulled through a window, which opened onto 'the yard'. A few escaped by making a bold dash from the veranda round and over the parapet. Two or three men were caught and assegaied as they attempted this. An Artilleryman named Howard, servant to Col. Harness, ran out of the Hospital and hid himself in the long grass growing on the bank outside. He covered himself with grass and twigs as well and quietly as he could and remained there all night. He came in unharmed at daylight, although the Zulus were around and about him all night. A small pig was shot dead by his side.

Sgt. Maxfield, a fine young soldier, was down with fever and delirious, he could not be moved and was killed in his bed.

The enemy now set fire to the roof of the Hospital. Being of thatch it blazed up at once. By its light our men were enabled to see their foes better and many fell before they retreated.

After a pause commanded or encouraged by an 'Induna' or Chief, who shouted his orders from time to time from the hill side, they came on again most pluckily, shouting their war cry 'Usutu'. The fighting now became desperate and in places hand-to-hand along the line of defence. The assailants used only their assegais and these as stabbing weapons; they seldom threw one. A soldier showing himself over the parapet was instantly thrust at, and this because the parapet was so low, and owing to their being no flanking fire, there were places where the Zulus could crouch beneath it in safety.

They even seized the bayonets and tried to wrench them from the muzzles of the rifles. One of our men to whom this happened had just loaded, he pulled the trigger and blew the plucky fellow to atoms.

At first the hurriedly made and rough lines of defence were constructed to hold a very much larger body of defenders than were actually engaged. A large number of natives and some white men having in the most cowardly manner deserted the post and bolted. Lt. Chard with admirable forethought and readiness of resource no sooner grasped this fact than he set men to construct a 'retrenchment' or inner line of defence connecting the corner of the store with the parapet on the garden side. This was made with biscuit boxes, and soon after the roof of the Hospital fell in our men had to take refuge inside this. Had he not done this it is probable that the Zulus would have rushed the position. The immediate safety of the little garrison being secured, Lt. Chard ably assisted by all available hands, constructed inside the inner lines what he termed a crow's nest of mealies sacks, and from which commanding position the fire of the defenders was rendered much more effective. Actg. Chaplain The

Revd. Geo. Smith of Estcourt, Natal, and Assistant Commissary Dunne contributed greatly to the construction and success of these little works. The enemy now endeavoured to fire the Store; one fine savage was shot by Corp. Attwood A.S. Corps as he was holding a lighted brand against the eaves. And so the fight continued till after midnight, from which time the attack gradually slackened, and the enemy carrying away with them as many of their dead and wounded as possible, according to their custom in battle, withdrew. Some days afterwards 50 large shields covered with blood were found by the riverside, showing where they had carried their dead and cast them into the river.

The last of them left just before dawn. The number composing the attack were estimated at 3,000. Many of the bodies by their shields and other distinctive marks, such as plumes, head gear, rings etc., etc., were identified as belonging to one of the King's chief and favourite regiments and one which bore a great reputation.

Our loss was 13 killed and 10 wounded; three of the latter died soon after of their wounds. Of the enemy we buried 370 and after a few days found over 100 more skeletons lying here and there in the long grass and bush between Rorke's Drift and the spot where they recrossed the Buffalo River. The larger proportion, in fact five out of six of the bodies found were those of old men, many of them quite wizened, and all spare and thin; a very few could be called fine men and only one or two approached 6 ft. The dead Zulus, especially those close round the post, were lying in the most distorted positions, some of them with their limbs almost tied in knots and with the appearance of dying hard and with great muscular contraction.

It behoves us now to mention the names of those who in this memorable defence especially distinguished themselves, and it must be understood that it was essentially a soldier's fight. Given all credit to the Officers who used the best judgement under the circumstances, and exhibited prompt action and readiness of resource; given also the confidence with which Lt. Chard and Bromhead, both young Officers, inspired their men, we repeat that it was a fight at odds of one white man to twenty black savages and more, frenzied with success and slaughter. Each individual soldier did his work and duty well. Ay' and right well.

No. 395 Pte. John Williams with the Joseph Williams before mentioned, was posted in the end room of the Hospital. They held it for more than an hour as long as they had a round left, but being unfortunately cut off from the rest of the Company they could get no more ammunition. After Joseph Williams was dragged out of the room

John Williams and two patients were the only ones left alive. The Zulus left them alone for a while to butcher Joseph Williams. Taking advantage of the lull, these men made a hole in the partition wall with an axe, and getting into the next room joined Pte. H. Hook who still at his post was covering the escape of the sick. John Williams and Hook, one working whilst the other kept the enemy at bay with his bayonet, cut holes through three other partitions and so working their way from room to room succeeding in getting all the remainder of the sick out through the window into 'The yard'. Pte. Hook was the last man to leave the Hospital and then it was in flames.

In another ward Pte. W. Jones and R. Jones had been placed by Lt. Bromhead. They defended their post to the last, and held the ward until 6 out of 7 of the patients entrusted to their charge had been safely removed. The seventh was Sgt. Maxfield. He was left for a while lying wounded on his bed. Pte. R. Jones giving up his rifle went back to try and carry him out. The room was full of Zulus, and he saw them stabbing the body on the bed. It was entirely owing to the pluck and exertions of these four men that the last of the patients escaped.

Actg. Commanding Officer Dalton, until badly wounded in the shoulder, and Cpl. Schiess N.N.C, a Swiss by birth, also wounded, deserve the highest praise for their cheerful encouragement of the soldiers and the good work they performed in the defence.

Cpl. W. Allen and Pte. Hitch 2/24th Regt must also be mentioned for their courageous work and assistance. It was chiefly due to these two men that communication was kept up with the Hospital at all. Holding at all costs a most dangerous post, raked in the reverse by the enemy's fire from the hill, they were both severely wounded, but their determined conduct enabled the patients to be withdrawn from the Hospital. When incapacitated from firing themselves, they continued as soon as their wounds had been dressed to serve out ammunition to their comrades during the night.

It was a gallant defence. The young soldiers backed each other up and fought splendidly; they never wavered for an instant. Most of them Welshmen by birth, by a few months of drill and training, and infusion of 'Esprit de Corps' had become the best and pluckiest of 'Warwickshire Lads' and gloriously upheld the traditions of the old 24th Regiment.

Again it was of the utmost strategical importance that this place should be held. It may almost be said that the safety of the remainder of the Column and at least of this part of the Colony depended on it.

When Lt. Gen. Lord Chelmsford left Rorke's Drift on the morning of the 24th of January 1879 for Pieter Maritzburg he desired Lt. Col. Degacher CB Commanding 2/24th Regt. to address the men of his Battalion at the first opportunity as follows: 'Not having time myself I wish to tell them how highly I think of their conduct it was admirable, no troops could have been steadier or more collected especially during the night of constant alarms, the 22nd, and although their conduct might be equalled it could not be surpassed. As for Lt. Bromhead and his Company nothing that I can now say can express my admiration of the gallant defence they made.'

Isandhlwana

I T remains now to be related what took place at the Camp at the Isandhlwana Hill.

The details have been collected from the few survivors who escaped.

About 7 a.m. the main Column being now out of sight, and far on its way down the Valley, the very enemy it had gone out to attack began to show themselves on the hills to the left front, or North East of the Camp. The outlying picquet for the day was found by 'G' Company of the 2/24th Regt. (the only Company of the Btn. left in Camp). It was Commanded by Lt. Pope and his men were extended in sections of fours in a line half a mile long with the right refused, and they covered the front of the right of the Camp; the N.N.C still further extended completing the cordon to the left. The sentries were ¼ of a mile from the Camp. The Officer Commanding the Native picquet reported the 1st appearance of the enemy. The bugles in the

1st 24th Regt. Camp sounded the 'Alarm' and the 'fall in'. The men turned out and with the two guns took up a central position in front of the 2/24th Camp. They so remained until a short time before 11 a.m., when as they had had no breakfast they were dismissed to get their breakfast and dinner together.

Col. Durnford RE in Command of a Rocket Battery, 5 Troops of Mounted Natives, recruited from the Basutos, and 250 native footmen had been sent for to the Camp in the morning from Rorke's Drift. Lt. Smith Dorrien 95th Regt. took the order, which was written by Col. North Crealock, Military Secretary to Lord Chelmsford – it ran: 'You are to strengthen the Camp and take Command of it.'

The Rocket Battery was under Capt. Russell RA and it was manned by a Bombardier RA and 8 men of the 1st 24th Regt.; the 3 tubes rockets and gear were carried on pack mules.

Col. Durnford rode in advance with 200 Basutos and arrived in Camp at about 10.45 a.m. He was now the senior Officer. Col. Pulleine on his arrival handed over the Command of the Camp to him at once, with the orders he had received from the Officer in Command of the Column, viz: 'To keep the men in Camp, act strictly on the defensive, extend the Cavalry and draw in the Infantry Picquets' or orders to this effect. It was further ordered that a mule wagon was to be ready loaded with ammunition to be sent out to the Column at a moment's notice if required, as they had taken no spare ammunition with them. Col. Durnford could be in no way justified in departing from these orders, neither could he divest himself of the responsibility of the Command. It is asserted by some that a difference of opinion or argument arose between these two Officers on this point, i.e. as to who was in Command.

It is certain that Col. Pulleine delivered the orders he had received to Col. Durnford immediately the latter arrived in Camp. The situation demanded unity of action and one fitted to assume the entire responsibility. Had Col. Durnford been the junior Officer the whole story of the battle might have to be otherwise written. To support this view the whole of the evidence tends to show that Col. Pulleine was prepared to act on the written instructions, and not to commit himself to any defensive (*sic*) movement. Had these orders been strictly adhered to, and carried out in their full meaning, the disastrous defeat we suffered must, humanly speaking, have been averted.

As before stated, the Forces left to act under these orders were considered ample for the defence of the Camp and of themselves.

A Glorious and decisive victory should have been gained by this small British Force over the countless hordes that poured on them.

That the Zulus might attack us under some such circumstances was the hoped for and express wish of every thinking man of the column.

Around the Camp fires we had said, 'With open ground in front, our reserve ammunition close at hand, and armed with such weapons as we have, if we cannot keep them from closing on us, the sooner we give up Africa and leave them the masters the better.'

What had been, might be. Forty years ago, viz; on the 16th December 1838 10 to 12,000 Zulus attacked 460 mounted Dutchmen in their entrenched Camp in Zululand. 3,000 Zulus fell after vainly assailing the Laager for 3 hours. The Dutchmen lost 5 killed and as many wounded. The then King Dingane burnt his Kraal, and fled with the remainder of his army, accepting this defeat as final and crushing. These Dutchmen then marched through Zululand and defeated every attack which they invariably awaited 'in Laager'. It is true and deeply to be regretted that in this case no attempt was made to thus defend this Camp. It was suggested by Col. Glyn, but deemed unnecessary as, 'it is not worthwhile and it will take too much time, and besides the wagons are most of them going back to Rorke's Drift for further supplies'. A more advantageous position we maintain for such a force as ours was, acting strictly on the defensive could not have been chosen or indeed well imagined. At the back the steep scarped face of the rock as a base, the summit and sides occupied by sharpshooters, the men and guns in an arc, or some other close formation, around this base in the front a sloping glacis, free for the most part of any obstacles (the whole of the tents might have been struck in two minutes by pulling away the poles), over which such a fire could have been poured, that had an enemy persisted in an attack, such a wall of dead would have been piled up that the living could not have surmounted it.

To return from what might have been to what actually happened.

We left Col. Durnford and Col. Pulleine in difference as to who was in Command. We will now show that they were of opposite opinions as to the tactics to be pursued. Whilst they were in consultation, a verbal report came in from the Officer Commanding the advanced native, Picquet. It was brought in by Lt. Adendorff of the N.N.C but as he was not understood Lt. Higginson N.N.C. was sent out for explanations. He brought the written answer to Col. Pulleine who ordered him to give it to Col. Durnford 'The Officer in Command'. Col. Durnford read it and said, 'Oh they are retreating are they, we must follow them up'. Capt. G. Shepstone, Col. Durnford's Staff Officer, with two troops of mounted Natives and accompanied by Capt. Barton had already been sent out to the direct left of the Camp, with orders 'to attack or follow up the enemy', they disappeared over the crest of the hill and must have at once become engaged, as rapid firing was heard from that direction. Col. Durnford desired Lt. Higginson to take Capt. Shepstone an order, 'to proceed with the Attack' and he was to lead, that he (Col. Durnford) with the Rocket Battery and remainder of Basutos, was proceeding more to the right, and that they were 'to endeavour to roll up the enemy between them'.

Lt. Higginson delivered the message and returned. When Col. Durnford had despatched this order, he asked Col. Pulleine to give him some Infantry; stated by Lt. Cochrane to be two Companies of the 1/24th Regt; to go out with him in support of the Rocket Battery. Col. Pulleine answered that '2 Companies could ill be spared but if ordered of course they must go', and he repeated the orders left him by Maj. Clery a second time. Col. Durnford said, 'Well I consider we ought to follow them up, I shall go off'. Col. Pulleine then promised that if he were hotly pressed he would send him a reinforcement.

Col. Durnford unable to see the proper tactics to be pursued, burning and impatient for the fray, and fretting at the curbing and restraining nature of the orders transmitted to him, left both the Camp and the direction of affairs.

It is well known that no braver Officer than Col. Durnford ever drew sword out of scabbard but, whether it was that his very courage drove him to the attack, or whether it was that some fancied slur or imputation rested on his name after the Langalibalele affair in the Bushman's Pass in 1873, which he was determined to wipe out, we know not. The result is the same. He was the senior and responsible Officer and it was not given to him to see the danger, or save the Camp and many, many very many precious lives.

Before he left the Camp 8 men came in from the South under a white flag of truce, and brought with them 11 guns. These they gave up and were allowed to depart to look after their cattle. This episode gave rise to a report that Col. Durnford had allowed some spies to visit and then leave the Camp.

Capt. G. Shepstone now rode in and reported to Col. Pulleine that the attack was much more serious than was at first imagined, that the enemy were coming on in great numbers. 'That the whole Zulu Army was advancing', that his Basutos though fighting splendidly were outnumbered and outflanked and were retreating, and he begged Col. Pulleine to send him out some support. Capt. Shepstone was pale and excited as he stated his wishes. He rode back to his death and told those with him, and those he met, that his report was laughed at and not believed. Col. Pulleine against his convictions and wishes, but forced by the urgency of this request from Col. Durnford's Staff Officer, ordered out two Companies of the 1/24th Regt. under Capt. Mostyn and Lt. Cavaye for this purpose. They advanced in echelon in attacking order a mile to the left and soon became engaged (the movements of these 2 Companies do not quite agree with those given by Capt. Essex 75th Regt. His account, though most clear and circumstantial, is not the same as that given by many other survivors). Just at this time, 11.30 a.m., the Officers sent in from the Column by Lord Chelmsford, arrived. The orders they brought perplexed Col. Pulleine greatly. What ought he to do?

Hours before, that is at 8.05 a.m., he had sent a despatch to the Officer Commanding the Column to say that the enemy were collecting and threatening the Camp. Now instead of the no doubt long looked for news that the Column was on its way to his succour, he is ordered to strike and send a large portion of the Camp out to the Column. The Oxen had before this been collected and tied to the 'trek chains' and Col. Pulleine ordered them to be in spanned and the General's orders to be executed, at the same time he sent the despatch marked 'L', in the first part of this narrative, to the General Commanding, and this was the last communication that passed between the Isandhlwana Camp and the main Column. The Officers' servants packed their masters tents and packed their things on the wagons, ready to move off.

The retreating movements of the enemy duly reported and before mentioned, must have been either a feint to draw out and extend our men, or an optical illusion consequent on their disappearing into and occupying two wooded Kloofs (or Ravines) and some dongas (deep water courses) that ran down from the hill. If the former was their object they succeeded admirably, and they now, just before noon, showed in far greater numbers all along the hills on the left and left front and poured down the slopes steadily and quickly in successive lines. This range of hills is called the Ingutu and the ridge for the whole of its length of 4½ miles was covered with black masses before they began to descend into the valley.

The 'fall in' sounded. The remaining 3 Companies of the 1/24th Regt. left in Camp with the two guns moved off 400 yds to the left and 'deployed into line'. The guns in line with the Infantry came at once into action, and getting the range committed great havoc with shrapnel. Bt. Maj. Smith RA was in Command of them.

Capt. Mostyn and Lt. Cavaye with their two Companies were gradually withdrawn and prolonged the line, the Company of the 2/24th Regt. on picquet had been withdrawn before this. They had been extended in sections of fours, and they retired on the right of the fighting line in admirable order, described 'as if on parade'. Up to this time these three advanced Companies had suffered no loss. As every word spoken by a combatant Officer during action is of interest as giving some clue to the progress of the fight, it may be mentioned, that Lt. Pope was heard to say that he considered himself fortunate in escaping part of his tour of picquet duty, that he and his Company had been 'warming them well out there, and that they would get it hotter directly'.

The enemy still advanced, clouds of skirmishers in front in lines of single rank with intervals, covering more compact bodies in rear. Our thin red line, well under cover, occupied the bed of the donga that ran a ¼ mile in front of the Camp, it kept up a terrific fire, and our foes were described as 'falling in heaps'. As those in front fell, others from behind were pushed into their places. They shouted out, 'You may shoot us down but we will trample you to death'. Every man that could hold a rifle and carry ammunition was ordered out of Camp and they all ran down and joined the fighting line in the Donga.

Presently the pack mules of the Rocket Battery came galloping in with their saddles underneath their bellies. Col. Durnford in his impatience had ridden with his two troops of mounted Basutos on ahead of the Battery, and he is said to have gone 5 miles trying to get round the enemy's left, but baffled by their numbers, he retired to find his Battery annihilated and his return by the way he had come cut off. Capt. Russell, whilst following him, was suddenly confronted by a body of Zulus when he came into action and fired 3 rockets from each tube at 600 yds range, and was then suddenly attacked by men who ran out of a Kloof only 100 yds to his left. The Zulus fired a volley and then rushed on the Battery, which so startled the mules that they became unmanageable and galloped off. The Bombardier

went after them and Capt. Russell was implored by his servant who was leading one of his horses and riding the other, to mount but while trying to do so he was shot. The 8 men of the 1/24th Regt. had 4 horses amongst them, 3 of them managed to escape, the other 5 and the mule drivers were all killed. The Zulus poured on over their bodies and trended away to their left and front. Col. Durnford got round them in rear, and with the men left to him, cut and forced his way back to Camp and joined the fighting line on its right. All accounts agree as to the admirable manner in which the Basutos, acting as Mounted Infantry, fought throughout the day.

At this time our men were holding their own and apparently keeping the enemy in check. This is said advisedly as although they kept the chest or body of the enemy stationary, the extension of the 'Horns' – their well-known tactic – was being carried out. In appearance they were now like a crescent with the centre 400 to 500 yards deep (a trooper who escaped describes the ground in front as 'being black with niggers'). Whilst the 'Horns' fed from the 'Chest' steadily continued to encircle the doomed Camp.

The movements of the right horn were concealed from view by the Isandhlwana hill, those on the left, to prevent our flank being turned, were met by an extension or opening out of our Infantry down the Donga to their right and further checked by the exertions of Col. Durnford and the mounted men with him. But few horsemen were seen with this part of their Army, though many were seen on the ridges watching the Battle. Our men now began running backwards and forwards by twos and threes for ammunition. Officers in Camp were serving it out and carrying it to the front.

Quartermaster Bloomfield 2/24th was shot dead in the performance of his duty. The enemy fired very quickly but with little effect; their bullets aimed at the men in the Donga went whistling high over and amongst the tents and a very few casualties occurred. The two guns continued to do good service. Maj. Smith for a while changed the position of one of the guns 200 yds to the right, and fired a few rounds to the front where there were some Kraals, but soon rejoined Lt. Curling, and the two guns concentrated their fire. They had fired about 40 rounds per gun, the last two cases at the enemy now distant only about 100 yds when suddenly the line ceased firing, turned about and began slowly to retire. In an instant, as a flash, the enemy who had been creeping nearer and nearer, heedless of the hundreds falling around them, dropped their guns and rushed forward with their assegais shouting, 'Usutu, Usutu'.

> *Usutu* is the Zulu name for Cetewayo's Army. In 1857, when he conquered his brother in a fight for the supremacy of the Kingdom, the victorious Army's cry was 'Luminylu Usutu'. Meaning the Usutu was overwhelmed. Since then Cetewayo's Army has been called the 'Usutu' and they have used the word for their Battle cry.

The scene instantly became one of the wildest and most awful descriptions. Many of the men had no time to fix their bayonets, but when mobbed and shooting was out of the question, in ones and twos and groups clubbed their rifles, and fought and died when they were caught and surrounded. To get together and rally under the rock or around the wagons, was the natural and prevailing idea, and some did get to the foot of the rock and fought to the last in mortal combat, whilst others rallied in two or more bodies near the 1/24th Regt. Camp, and there fell in heaps of 50 and 60, but the British soldier sewn up in uniform carrying a rifle, his feet encased in heavy boots, his body hampered in straps and pouches, had no chance in a race with the naked savage, his dress a feather or two and his weapons a slight shield and spear. Man to man we must have crushed them in this final struggle, outnumbered by 20 to one it was hopeless.

Had our men remained in the scattered and extended position that they had held for the last hour without any kind of reserve, the same result must have inevitably happened.

On the left the men were somewhat closer, especially on the crest of a slight rise at the head of the Donga, but in the Donga itself there were as many as ten paces between the files. What could these men have done against the rush of vast numbers?

In ten minutes there was not a white man left alive in Camp, not one was spared, not a prisoner taken, as soon as a man fell he was thrown on his back, ripped open by the stabbing assegai, and otherwise mutilated. It is the Zulu custom to thus treat a slain enemy, a superstition preserved and inculcated by their Witch doctors, who tell them that if they neglect this precaution, they themselves will die of a swollen belly. Many of the bodies were found tied with 'Rheims' or strips of rawhide, by the hands and feet, but it is doubtful if this was done for the purpose of torture. We believe that all mutilation was done in sheer glut of blood after death.

Most of the bodies were more or less stripped, one little band boy of the 2/24th Regt., a negro child, was hung by the heels to the tail of an ox wagon and his throat cut. Even the dogs and goats about the Camp and the horses and mules tied to the picquet rope were butchered. Further details would be too sickening.

What made the line retire will be asked and in answer the evidence is conflicting in the extreme. Two survivors say that they distinctly heard bugles sound 'the cease fire' and 'Retire' and that it was passed down the line, others and the majority say they heard nothing of this. That the 'cease fire' should have sounded seems hardly credible, but the 'retire' would account for the movement. We believe that the bugles did sound the retire on the left, but whether the buglers got an order to sound or who gave it, is a mystery that will never be solved. It can only he surmised that some Officer, seeing the danger at last of opposing an attack formation, against an attack, where collective and defensive measures should only have been used, gave the order to retire, and the Company Officers and the men seeing their danger reluctantly gave up their position in the Donga and tried to get together and rally.

It will be here necessary to examine and note the last observed incidents that happened before the final rush of the enemy, and to account more fully if possible for the disastrous result. The universal testimony is that up to the last moment no one believed for an instant that there was the slightest danger of the Camp being taken, that there was no sign of hesitation, no fear for the result, no thought of wavering, that everyone kept steadily to his work of firing and fighting. In the first place then, the men had been firing hard and fast for nearly an hour, they commenced with 70 rounds per man, and these must have been pretty well expended. The reserve was in the wagons, at the nearest point 500 yds in rear, every available man was in the ranks and there were no arrangements made for bringing up the cartridges to the fighting line, and therefore as has been already stated the men had to renew their supply by running back to the wagons themselves. From this it is clear that our soldiers were getting short of ammunition and that there was some confusion and difficulty in getting more. Again there were some hundreds of the N.N.C. in Camp, many of them dressed or partially so in coats and other castaway clothing, whilst each man wore to distinguish him from the Zulus, a piece of red cloth tied round his hat or head. With the exception of one strong Company out on picquet they had not taken any part in the fight, but were ordered to remain drawn up in Column of Companies in rear of their own tents ready to be slipped at the foe when defeated. As the said foe approached nearer and nearer, terror entered into their souls, the inborn fear of the hated and terrible Zulu possessed them, their Officers could scarcely control them, and at last breaking all restraint they stripped off their clothes and red pugarees, hoping thereby to escape detection, and bolted 'en masse'.

What finally drove them to flight was doubtless the sight of their comrades, the one Company just mentioned, flying before the advancing Zulu chest, and as this Company occupied though farther in advance, the central position of our line of defence, as it broke and fled it left a gap in the line through which the closely pursuing enemy poured into the

Camp. The direction these men of the N.N.C. took was right up our Camp, then up by the nek between the Isandhlwana hill and the Kopje. There finding the road to Rorke's Drift blocked by the right horn of the enemy they made straight for the river.

This stampede occurred just as the buglers sounded the 'retire', and it is more than probable that our own men were unable to distinguish between these men and Zulus, more especially as they were closely pursued, and at the same time the enemy showed themselves round the back of Isandhlwana and the excitement was complete.

It is impossible to arrive at a correct estimate of the numbers of the enemy who attacked the Camp, or of their loss in the battle, but after taking every report and observation into consideration, it may be concluded that not less than 15,000 must have been engaged, whilst 5,000 men were held in reserve, and that their loss was very heavy indeed. To increase the difficulty in counting this loss we know that the Zulus will not allow the numbers of their killed in battle to be counted, and for this reason after a victory they always carry off and bury their dead. If left over night or for many hours they will not touch a dead body, not even of their own people.

That the loss in killed both at Isandhlwana and Rorke's Drift was most severe was confirmed by reports that afterwards came in from Zululand. One stated the Zulu nation had been 'assegaied in the belly', meaning that it had received a mortal wound. Another, 'that there were not tears enough to weep for the dead'. Another report generally stated and confirmed by King Cetewayo himself, was that they had lost more men at Isandhlwana than at all the other battles, Kambula and Ginginhlove (*sic*) included.

After taking the Camp the enemy had several hours of daylight in which to loot it undisturbed. They did this thoroughly, removing or destroying everything. Some of the tents they burnt, but most they cut up into strips, wherewith to remove their dead, two men carrying four bodies. A native wagon driver who was wounded and remained till night and then hobbled across the river, says that he saw 40 wagon loads of corpses, and he also described how they removed their dead in long strips of canvas. Their chief booty was upwards of 1,000 M.H. rifles, 350 to 400,000 rounds of ammunition, 2 guns, 120 weapons , £20,000 worth of trek oxen, blankets, stores of all descriptions, and all our personal belongings.

The colours of the 2/24th Regt. having been left in Camp, in the Guard tent were lost, every soul of the Btn. viz; 5 Officers and 178 men left in Camp having been killed. It was at first feared that the

1/24th Regt. had also lost their Queen's Colour, the only one they had with the Headquarters, the Regimental Colour having been left at Helpmakaar with the left half Battalion.

A most gallant and successful attempt to save the Queen's Colour was made by Lt. Melville the Adjutant of the Regiment, when the Zulus made their first charge and so encompassed our men that their fate was hopeless; a desperate attempt was made by some of the mounted Officers and men and a few others from the right rear to the hill towards the Buffalo River 4 miles distant. The N.N.C. has as been written led the way, the ground was covered with loose boulders and stones, and so uneven and broken that the enemy on feet were able to keep up with, and in many cases pass those on horseback. The few white men who started on foot were quickly despatched none getting more than ½ mile from Camp.

By the traces found afterwards these showed that they had sold their lives dearly, their bodies been found in groups, round trees and other rallying points with signs of the struggle they had made all about them. Those that were mounted rode for their lives and some got away. Lt. Melville seeing that all was over, seized the colour and galloped off. Before reaching the river he was joined by Lt. Coghill ADC also of the 1/24th Regt. These two agreed to stick together and save the colours whatever happened.

They reached the river bank and plunged in, the bed where they crossed was very rocky, and the water rushed through in channels, now deep, now shallow. The river is here 40 yds wide and on this day numbers of friends and foes were washed away in the current, Lt. Coghill got across; Lt. Melville, though a famous horsemen was washed against a boulder, onto which his horse attempted to scramble, so plunged, and reared, that, hampered as he was with the colour, it threw him, and he was carried downstream towards another rock to which Lt. Higginson NHC was clinging. Lt. Melville cried out to him to catch hold of the colour, and he did so, but the pace that Lt. Melville was coming down stream washed Lt. Higginson off the rock and both of them into deep and comparatively still water. Here they were obliged to let go the colour and Lt. Coghill rode back to their assistance. His horse was shot dead by a bullet in the forehead as it stepped into the water by the Zulus, who were lining the opposite bank and keeping up a rapid fire at Lt. Melville who had on a scarlet jacket. It is remarkable that it was against the 'red soldiers' that the Zulus expended all their fury, and during the fight there were instances of those in blue, or other coloured coats, being passed and even pushed aside to enable them to get at the men dressed in scarlet, and several of those who escaped ascribed it entirely to their not being dressed in our national colour.

These three Officers, however, got to land on the Natal side of the Buffalo. They were greatly exhausted, partly from the quantity of water they had swallowed, and partly from their struggles in the river. For a moment they laid down on the water's edge and then getting over the first 200 yards of the bank which is flat, they began with difficulty to climb the side of the ravine which was exceedingly steep. Lt. Coghill was lame from an old injury to his knee, and on this account had been left in Camp that day. They had gone but a little way up when they saw that the Zulus were crossing after them.

They scrambled on till Lt. Coghill said, 'I am done; I can go no further.' Lt. Melville said, 'Neither can I.' Lt. Higginson begged them to shoot as they still had their revolvers, he having lost his rifle in the river, went on, and at the top of the bank found some Basutos who were keeping up a fire on the advancing Zulus, and trying to cover the retreat of the Officers. Lt. Higginson and the Basutos waited a little while, as long as they dared stop without fear of their being surrounded, and rode off. Worn out and faint with their exertions, Lt. Melville and Coghill were unable to climb the last 30 yds to safety, and were caught up and shot or assegaied by their inexorable pursuers. Could they have climbed this last short distance they would have been able to have got away with the Basutos as the latter had secured 3 stray ponies.

A week afterwards their bodies, happily not mutilated, were found lying close together about 700 yds from the river's edge. They had perished assisting each other as true comrades in a heroic attempt to save the treasured standard of their Regt. Both fine young accomplished Officers, and favourites with all who knew them, their falling when so nearly saved, was one of the saddest incidents of this dreadful day.

On the 4th February, 13 days afterwards, Maj. Black 2/24th Regt. with a small party of volunteers, rode from Rorke's Drift and buried the two bodies where they fell. The Revd. G. Smith read the burial service. On the 14th April in the presence of Col. Glyn and Degacher and numerous Officers of both Battalions, their bodies were exhumed, placed in coffins, and buried five yards from the place where they were first found. A memorial cross presented by Sir. B. Frere was placed on a rock just above the graves, with the following inscription:

'In Memory of Lt. and Adjt. T. Melville and Lt. N.G.A. Coghill 1st Btn., 24th Regiment

who died on this spot, 22nd January
1879, to save the Queen's Colour of their
Regiment.' And on the reverse ,'Jesu mercy.
For Queen and Country.'

Maj. Black and his party on the 4th February, next
proceeded to look for the lost Colour. Fortune
favoured them, and 500 yds below the crossing
place, first the case, and then the crest (Lion and
Crown) which fits on the top of the Staff were
found; and 5 yds below these the Colour in rags,
was lying in the water. Capt. Harford N.N.C. found
the Colour and Lt. Trowe of the same Regt., the
crest. Neither would have been found had not the
river gone down 3 ft at the least since the day on
which they were lost.

The Colour was brought back in triumph to
Rorke's Drift and received with cheer upon cheer by
the men of the 2/24th Regt., who manned the walls
of the laager. Maj. Black rode in with it through the
gateway and handed it to Col. Glyn CB who, when a
Major of the 1/24th, first received it on presentation
by Lady Wodehouse at the Curragh in 1867. Col.
Glyn handed it to Col. Degacher saying, 'I entrust
it to you and your Battalion for safe keeping'. The
next day it was taken to Helpmakaar, and received
with cheers and the greatest enthusiasm by the two
Companies 1/24th Regt. there stationed.

Lt. Smith Dorrien, 95th Regt., acting Transport Officer had a marvellous escape. He rode off from the battlefield on a tired horse. On the top of the precipitous bank, overlooking the river he was begged by a mounted Infantry soldier, who was wounded and had his horse killed under him to tie up his arm, as he was bleeding to death.

He dismounted and did so making a tourniquet of his pocket handkerchief and riding stick. Just now Maj. Stuart Smith RA passed them and he had been badly wounded in the arm before going out of action, he told Lt. Smith Dorrien to be quick as the enemy were upon them. Poor Maj. Smith weak and faint from loss of blood, fell whilst leading his horse down the bank and was killed at the bottom. He had changed horses with a Sgt. of his own Battery for some unaccountable reason just after starting. The Sgt. rode in to Helpmakaar with Maj. Smith's regulation cape rolled and strapped on the pommel of the saddle, it was riddled with distinct marks of bullets and assegai thrusts. Before Lt. S. Dorrien could mount his horse again, it was stabbed and he rushed down the bank and into the river, and being luckily washed within reach of a horse that was swimming across, caught it by the tail, and was towed across.

On landing he was too exhausted to secure the animal and it broke away, but he managed to escape on foot and reached Helpmakaar 14 miles away, dead beat but saved.

Others had similar incidents in their escapes, and it is worthy of note that not a single wounded white man escaped from Isandhlwana.

It is stated and seems beyond question, that several of our people were killed on the way to the river, and more on the banks by Zulus whose submission Lord Chelmsford had accepted, and who had received permission to return to their Kraals, which lay along the route taken by the fugitives.

We left the two guns firing case shot at 100 yds range. When the Infantry retired the guns, which it must be remembered were worked in line with it, were ordered to 'Limber up'. Before they could overtake the retiring line, the Zulus were on them stabbing the gunners in the back as they held on to the carriages and endeavouring to mount the limbers. This point is important as showing how close the enemy had got to our line, and how quick their rush must have been.

As the guns retired through the Camp they had no further opportunity of coming into action, the whole place being a seething mass of black and white combatants, the guns could only advance at a slow trot. Soldiers of all arms held on to the gun carriages, ran alongside and were killed as they ran. One gun was taken before it reached the neck. Maj.

Smith, who led the other when he saw that he could not get down the road to Rorke's Drift, turned off to the left with the other fugitives. The ground soon became impassable for wheels and the gun upset.

The enemy were on them in a moment, stabbed the horses in the traces, and killed the drivers, who having nothing with which to defend themselves fell an easy prey. Maj. Smith and Lt. Curling rode off. The fate of the first named good, and most rising young Officer, we have already written. The other, more fortunate, got away.

Five Officers only of the Imperial Amy who were present at the fight lived to tell the tale as they saw it, viz; Capt. Essex 75th Regt., Capt. Allen Gardner 14th Hussars, Lt. Cochrane 32nd Regt., Lt. Curling RA and Lt. Smith Dorrien 95th Regt. About 30 other Officers and men of the different mounted branches, and an unknown number of natives escaped.

The 24th Regt. lost 21 officers and 583 men and besides these 27 other Officers and about 240 white men soldiers and others, perished at their post, all gallantly upholding the character of Englishmen, who, though they could not conquer, knew how to die. In the whole of English history we cannot find a parallel to this terrible loss in one single day.

Once more to review the causes of this fatal disaster, even now most difficult thoroughly to understand. First, we have the great and unpardonable neglect of any precautions to Laager the Camp. Then we have the very questionable policy of dividing the force to attack an unknown enemy of unknown strength. The easy, too easy, success and this false experience of the just concluded Kaffir war in the Cape Colony, may have something to say to this. In any case there is no doubt whatever that the power of the Zulus was completely underrated.

Next we have Col. Durnford against his possible orders 'to strengthen the Camp and act on the defensive' both leaving the Camp himself and instituting offensive movements for which the little force was nor calculated to act.

Again we have the extension and scattering of our soldiers without any reserve when the only safety lay in keeping them together in the closest formation.

These, with the failing of the ammunition and the presence of the N.N.C, an undoubted source of weakness, together make up the battle of Isandhlwana on the 22nd January 1879, and which will be remembered for ever as a black letter day in the history of our empire.

In conclusion let us quote the words of an Officer who was out with the Generals' Column on the 22nd, and who said after we returned to Rorke's Drift the next day, 'Thank God it was no worse'.

List of survivors
1/24th Regt.

Pte. Williams.	Groom to Col. Glyn.
Pte. Bickley	Band.
Pte. Wilson	Band
Pte. Trainer	Rocket Battery
Pte. Johnson	Rocket Battery
Pte. Grant	Mounted Infantry
And one man	Mounted Infantry

Officers who escaped

Capt. Essex	75th Regt.
Capt. Gardner	14th Hussars
Lt. Cochrane	32nd Regt.
Lt. Smith Dorrien	95th Regt.
Lt. Curling	RA

Statements by survivors

Statement of No. 139. Pte. J. Williams 1/24th Regt. (Groom to. Col. Glyn)

On the 22nd January 1879. I was called up at 2 a.m. to get Col. Glyn's horse ready, he started about 4.0 a.m., with the patrol under the Lt. Gen. I remained in Camp to look after the Colonel's other two horses about 9 a.m. a mounted orderly came in to report Zulus on the hills to the left of the Camp. He made his report to Lt. Coghill at the Column Office; that Officer went to Col. Pulleine to inform him. The Column alarm was then sounded and the 5 Companies of the 1/24th Regt. fell in, and the Company of the 2/24th Regt. The Artillery harnessed their horses. The Column was marched below the N.N.C. camp where they waited for orders for about ½ an hour. They were then sent back to their own Camp where they stood under arms about ¾ of an hour after which Col. Pulleine gave them permission to fall out without taking off their accoutrements. During this time Zulus were visible to the left front, sometimes in small numbers, at others in large bodies. The 'fall in' was sounded a second time about 11 o'clock, and the column was formed up in the same spot as before, below the space between the 2/24th and N.N.C. Camps. The Zulus were now advancing on the Camp along the top of the hills, to the left. Col. Durnford's column had come in by this time, and his party went out of Camp towards our left front, some ¾ of a mile off, and went round a small conical hill, No. 5 Company 1/24th was sent to the left in skirmishing order, to support some N.N.C. who were already there. As soon as Col. Durnford's mounted party were out of sight we heard firing from their direction, but could not tell whether it was from them or the end, and five minutes afterwards the party on the left were engaged and we could see masses of Zulus coming over the hills in that direction. No. 1 Company was now sent out in support of Col. Durnford and the guns commenced firing on the Zulus as they came down the hills to our left, and left front, with great effect, and the Zulus began to retreat behind the hill Col. Durnford had gone round, his party having commenced to retire on its supports. The enemy occupied some Kraals which were to the right of the hill, but were driven out by the Artillery fire, when they extended in skirmishing order to the right should say from two to three hundred yds deep, they then advanced round towards the right of the Camp, outflanking the mounted men who were extended that side. Meanwhile, there was very heavy firing on the left and left centre. I myself and Pte. Hough the Cols. Cook, went to the left beyond the Generals' Camp where we were joined by three of the General's servants, and began to fire from the left of No. 5 Co. 1/24th Regt. We fired 40 or 50 rounds each when the N.N.C. fell back on the Camp and one of their Officers pointed out to me that the enemy were entering the right of the Camp.

We then went to the right, No. 5 Co., still holding its position, and fired away the remainder of our ammunition. The Zulus turned to the left of No. 5 Coy, by coming over a high rock, the firing at this point still continued very heavy. Meanwhile No. 5 Co. and the remainder of the 1st & 2nd 24th, were firing volleys into the Zulus who were only 100 or 150 yds from them. They kept this up till they got short of ammunition. The right of the Camp was open and undefended except by the few mounted troops left in Camp, who had taken cover in a small ravine. The Zulus kept outside the Camp some 200 or 300 yds and made it round to the right completely surrounding the Camp except a small space to the left of the road to Rorke's Drift.

The men in Camp, Bandsmen, and men on guard were trying to take ammunition to the Companies but the greater part never got there. I saw horses with ammunition on their backs galloping about Camp a short time afterwards. Lt. Coghill galloped up now to the Colonel's tent and ordered them to be struck and placed in the wagon which was done, when he came up again and ordered the grooms to take the horses to the part of the Camp. I kept one of the Col's horses tied to the wagon and went and get 40 rds more ammunition of which I used 29 rounds, I then saw Lt. Melville leaving Camp with the Queen's Colour and Lt. Coghill close behind him, the latter told me to come on or I should get killed. Just then the two guns of the RA retreated out of Camp past me, I saw the men on foot who had attempted to escape turned back and coming into camp. When I got onto the hill overlooking the Rorke's Drift road the Zulus were entering the Camp from that direction and I saw Lt. Coghill's horse assegaied in the hip. About 300 yds outside the Camp the ground became so bad that the guns of the RA were upset and I saw several of the drivers assegaied. I passed them here and saw no more of the guns. On my way to the drift I passed Band Sgt. Gamble on foot but could give him no assistance. When I got down to the drift I saw Lt. Coghill and Melville coming down the rocks to it and after I entered the river to cross I saw no more of either of these Officers, I made my way up to Helpmakaar after crossing the river.

Statement of No. 1178. Pte. G. Bickley, Band 1/24th Regt.

At about 7 a.m. on the 22nd January 1879, one of the Volunteers who had been away from Camp on picquet duty came in and made a report to the Commanding Officer. I immediately after this heard Mr. Melville give an order to the bugler to sound the 'fall in' and add sound the 'Column call'. Each Corps fell in opposite its own Camp and the picquets were then brought in consisting of a Company of each Btn. 24th Regt. The Infantry formed up in an open space between the Camps of the 2/24th and the RA At this time I was posted as a picquet sentry on the Officers Mess, all the servants having fallen in with their Companies. About half an hour after the Column had fallen in Col. Durnford's mounted Basutos were sent up a hill to our left, at the time we could see with field glasses Zulus on the hills to our left quite distinctly. Cetewayo's half brother in charge of same.

One of the N.N.C. came in soon after and in my hearing reported himself to Col. Pulleine as having come off picquet, and obtained permission to bring in some of his men from the rear of the hill behind the Camp. About this time a second mounted messenger was sent out to bring in a party working on the road under Lt. Anstey, which came in some ¾ of an hour afterwards. After waiting under arms for some hour and a half to two hours the men were dismissed with orders not to take off their accoutrements. Very shortly afterwards we had been dismissed we heard very heavy firing from the hill on the left where the Basutos had been sent, and immediately the 'fall in' sounded the 2nd time, and No. 5 Company 2/24th was sent soon afterwards on to the hill to support the Basutos. By the time the Column was formed up the Basutos were coming down the ridge pursued by the Zulus and the Company 2/24th had opened fire. The Rocket Battery under Col. Durnford was also engaged at this time about a mile from our left front. The guns opened fire about this time, one on the Zulus coming down the ridge on our left flank and the other on those advancing on Col. Durnford's party to our left front. The Mounted Police and one Company 1/24th Regt. was sent out after this in support of Col. Durnford's party. The gun firing in this direction appeared to have great effect and soon after it began firing they made a retreat, but afterwards they reappeared in extended order coming over the rise to the left front and near a conical hill. At the same time a line of Zulus appeared right across a plain in front of the Camp, completely outflanking that of our skirmishers, and there were Kraals on both sides of the Camp which were occupied by the Zulus. Our men began to retire on the Camp, making a stand in a ravine which crossed the front of the Camp. The Companies out skirmishing were now apparently getting short of ammunition and it was being carried out to them by the Bandsmen, wagon drivers and other unarmed people about the Camp. The N.N.C had been driven into Camp and together with most of the Transport and other employed natives were rushing out of Camp towards the road to Rorke's Drift.

The Quartermaster then came up and asked me if I could saddle his horse for him. I took it behind the wagon near the Officers Mess to do so, but could find no bridle. I left the horse tied up to the wagon by the headstall but saw no more of the Quartermaster who had gone away in another direction.

By this time all the idlers were clearing out of Camp and the skirmishers had been driven in, I made for the nek over which the road ran and on gaining it saw that retreat by the road to Rorke's Drift was cut off, and so struck off to the left. About a ¼ mile on I found a pony standing in the path which I mounted and shortly afterwards caught up Lt. Melville who was carrying the 'Queen's Colour'.

Mr. Coghill afterwards joined us and reported to the Adjutant that Col. Pulleine had been shot. Cpl. Richardson came up soon after and said he had been wounded in the arm, and soon afterwards I saw him fall off his horse and lie on the ground unable to remount.

When I got down to the drift I could see nothing of the Officers who had passed me. From the drift I found my way with Capt. Essex , whom I met at the top of the hill, to Helpmakaar.

Statement by No. 15, Pte. E. Wilson Band 1/24th Regt.

I was in the Band and in the Camp of the 1/24th Regt, at Isandhlwana on the 22nd January 1879. The Regt. fell in at about 8 o'clock the 'fall in' going while we were at breakfast, and marched to the Camp of the 2/24th Regt. The Bandsmen were all told off as stretcher bearers and fell in with the Regt. The remainder (boys etc) remaining in Camp. The Regt. remained under arms up to 10.50 a.m. when Col. Durnford came in. Soon after 'E' Company (Lt. Cavaye) moved out to the left. The remainder were marched back to our own parade ground and dismissed with orders not to take off our accoutrements.

We were told to get our dinners as quickly as possible and be in readiness to fall in at any moment. The 'fall in' sounded about ¼ of an hour afterwards, and the Regt. marched off to the left front of the Camp. I myself went to the Hospital tent to get a stretcher. While I was on my way to rejoin my Company I first heard firing on the hills to the left of the Camp. I could not at this time see anything of 'E' Company which was out of sight. The Guns were in action, one firing to the left and one to the left front of the Camp. 'A' Company 1/24th was lying in support in rear of them. I was going to join this Company but was ordered by the Doctor to join the 4 Companies remaining on the parade ground. Some ten minutes afterwards these Companies were sent out to the front of the Camp in skirmishing order. The stretcher bearers were out with their Companies for some ten minutes, when we were ordered by Dr. Sheppard to go to the Hospital tents as he said there would be too many wounded for us to attend to. As we were going there ammunition was beginning to be brought to the Companies. While in the Hospital tent I saw the hills to the left and in front covered with Zulus advancing on the Camp. To the right some of the Police Carbineers and the N.N.C were engaged very hotly and retiring on the Camp. They made a stand for some time in a sluit which crossed the front of the Camp, but were driven out of it after ¼ of an hour or 20 minutes.

The idlers and men in among the tents were now making the best of their way out of Camp. The Doctor told us we were no longer likely to be of any use, and the Band Sergeant told us we had better get away as best we could. I with another man began to retire on a hill in rear of the Camp taking a stretcher and followed the men who had gone before towards the Buffalo. About ¾ mile from Camp I caught a horse and rode down to the river where I lost him in crossing. Some 50 or 100 yds on the Natal side I met Pte. Bickley. Further on I got a horse from a Volunteer and rode up to Helpmakaar where I arrived about 7.20 p.m. in Company with Sgt. Morton Mounted Infantry.

Mr. Brickhill's statement. Interpreter to Col. Glyn
On the morning of 22nd January 1879 between 6 and 7 o'clock the Zulus in considerable force at the South end of the Ingutu Hills shortly afterwards another force came in sight at about the middle of the Ingutu and the intervening space was quickly filled in. We took a hasty breakfast and then all hands were ordered to prepare for action, the cooks also being ordered to take their places in the ranks. At least I heard this order given to the cooks of 1/24th Regt. All the forces were drawn up in front of the 2/24th Regt. and N.N.C. Camps and there remained until 12.30 p.m. Between 8 and 9 o'clock

8 natives came in from the South of the Camp under a white flag. They brought in 11 guns in satisfaction of the demands made on them by H.E. the General on the previous day. I took them to the Column Office and from there to Col. Durnford at the back of the N.N.C. Camp. The Col. seemed quite glad to see me, came forward and shook hands heartily (I had only met him once before, 12 months ago when the Tugela postmaster being confined to bed with fever I superintended the punting of the Escort, baggage etc., accompanying the Zulu border Commissioners).

He asked what I was there when one of the 1/24th Regt. Officers told him I was Interpreter to Col. Glyn's Column. He seemed disappointed as though he would have liked me to have been with him. The natives then asked leave as the General was not there, to go back and collect their cattle which had strayed away to their old pastures on the flats above Whlarakari and said they would return next day. Col. Durnford asked me whether I thought it was all right. I replied that I knew some of the men then present had come to the General under a flag of truce on the previous day and that I saw no reason to mistrust them. He accordingly allowed the men to go, and they went by the way they came. I am particular in stating this because a report has gained some credence to the effect that

Col. Durnford had allowed a lot of Zulu spies to come in and go out of Camp on the morning of the fight, without let or hindrance, and that they went and joined the enemy. All that passed was conveyed through me, they were marched in and out under a guard. I took them along the back of the Camp, so that they should not know too much about our force ranged in front, and the whole thing took so short a time, that even if they had been spies they could have gained no information which would have benefited the Zulu Army if they had joined it, which, however, they did not, for they fled across into Natal, that same afternoon amongst our refugees.

Between 9 and 10 o'clock I ordered all the wagoners to collect their oxen, which were then scattered all round the Camp and might impede the action of the troops, and tie them to the yokes but not inspect them. As I returned I took Col. Pulleine's word that 2 bodies of Durnford's horse were signalled as approaching along the Rorke's Drift road. I came back through a corner of the Carabineers Camp where I met Capt. Bradstreet and Messrs Moody Bulrock & London. We stood there listening to what we thought was the General engaged with the enemy. We could almost have sworn that we heard rapid artillery firing, then volleys of small arms, then single shots. Afterwards the firing seemed to come from a more Northerly direction than the General could have possibly been, so we concluded that General Woods' Column had come up and was engaging another portion of the enemy. This illusion (for such it proved to be) was caused by the echoes and reverberations from the surrounding hills of a lot of small arms discharged by the N.N.C. and Volunteers at a number of small parties of the enemy forming the decoy at the head of the Mangeni Valley.

At 10.30 Durnford's horse arrived, a welcome addition indeed to our meagre forces. At about 11 o'clock a party of them were sent back by the way they came round the Isandhlwana and from there round the Northernmost part of the Ingutu, to check the enemy's secret advance in that direction, for those in the middle of the Ingutu had disappeared again over the hill. At nearly 12 o'clock the rest of Durnford's Horse were sent to attack the Zulus now collected in large numbers on the Southernmost part of Ingutu. I had no field glass and cannot say whether the Rocket Battery accompanied them. They went round to tile right of the conical hill and attacked the Zulus at the Southern nek. We heard heavy firing over the Northern neck, down which directly afterwards three horsemen came at full speed, Capt. G. Shepstone, who was one of them, rode into the 1/24th Regt. Camp and asked for the Officer in Command. I was taking him to Col. Pulleine's tent when one of our Officers shouting the Colonel's name came out, but before Capt. Shepstone could recover his breath to speak to him, Capt. Gardner of the General's Staff rode up with a letter from the General, which the Colonel read aloud, only four of us present. It was an order to strike the Camp, and come on with all speed leaving a sufficient guard behind to protect such as could not be moved without delay. Capt. Shepstone then said, 'I am not an alarmist Sir, but the Zulus are in such black masses over there, such long black lines, that you will have to give us all the assistance, you can, they are now fast driving our men this way.'

As he spoke the Basutos (Durnford's Horse) came retiring over the Northern neck, keeping up a steady fire as they retreated before the Zulus. Capt. Gardner then said to Col. Pulleine who seemed undecided as to what he ought to do 'under the circumstances I should advise your disobeying the General's order for the present at any rate the General knows nothing of this he is only thinking of the cowardly way in which the Zulus are running away from our troops over yonder'. They went away together. I caught and saddled my horse, and then having no weapon of my own went about the Camp in the hopes of getting one somewhere and joining in the fight. In this I failed so I betook myself to a

88

fairly commanding position in front of the Column Office. I found the whole Army drawn out in Battle array to the extreme left of the Camp under the Ingutu, Durnford's horse were holding the plain to the left of the Northern neck, the white mounted force to its right, the two field pieces a little behind and between them. The Infantry were in line in rear about a mile from the nearest Camp. The whole 4-mile length of the Ingutu was by this time covered by Zulus. They kept up a continuous fire upon our men, but appeared to me to shoot at too great a distance for their fire to be effective. The Durnford's Horse were now drawing the enemy down Southern nek in great numbers. These on the Northern neck retired to a crest in the nek which joins the Isandhlwana to Ingutu. Leaving their horses well sheltered here they held the crest splendidly keeping up a steady galling fire which, with that of the counted white force on the right, checked what was at first a very determined advance in the direction of Camp, and instead of coming on they passed over the northernmost end of Ingutu. The Artillery threw about 25 shots from the different parts of the field during the Battle. Four of these were very effective, each tearing up what appeared to be about an acre of ground in the enemy's masses. One of the guns appeared to shoot high, whilst one shot burst halfway, nearly over the N.H.C. Durnford's Horse now appeared to the right of the conical hill, keeping up a steady fire and retreating parallel to the road to Mangeni Valley. A much larger force now confronted them, than we had yet seen, showing that the enemy had had large accessions to his strength, from the hidden end of Ingutu behind conical hill.

The mounted white force now went down to their assistance and these together held the plain so determinedly, that the Zulu line actually wavered once, and they sought to mass together under cover of a Kraal in front of conical hill. A well-placed shot from one of the field pieces caused considerable havoc and scattered them from there. A general forward movement was now made by the enemy from the Kraal just named, right up to Northern nek. This was opposed by the two guns and the Infantry alone, the N.N.C had left and passed through the Camp one determination seemed settled on them viz, to escape.

I could see nothing of the details of the Infantry fighting because of the low lying ground, but if the unceasing roll they kept up was any indication at all then the enemy's losses must have been heavy indeed. Our mounted force was now compelled to retire on a gully. The Zulus left horn having already extended two miles below the road to Mangeni Valley. They did not come on in lines but evenly distributed. Nowhere could you catch three men walking together and rarely two so that in some places their front was sometimes ¾ of a mile in front of their rear.

The Gully the Mounted Police and others held most tenaciously every shot appearing to take effect, so much so, that with the havoc caused by the shell thrown into the Kaffir Kraal before mentioned 1,000 Zulu dead must have lain between the conical hill and the gully.

They lay just like peppercorns upon the plain. The leading Zulus finding they were being mown down so terribly threw themselves down flat on the ground to wait for the others to come up when they jumped and came on again. One of Durnford's Horse now brought up a wounded companion sitting on the horse behind him. Our mounted men now made for their horses. The Zulus took advantage of this slight break and pushed across the gully sharply whilst their left horn drew in slightly towards the Camp. A simultaneous forward movement was now made by all the Zulus and many of our mounted men who had ridden in for ammunition were closely followed in by them. Men were new running towards Rorke's Drift. Going down to the 1/24th Regt. Camp I saw Mr. Dubois who asked me in Zulu how I thought it looked, I said 'Ugly' he then said, yes the enemy has scattered us this day. In the Camp I saw Quartermaster Pullen, he tried to rally some of the men shouting, 'Follow me and let us try to turn the enemy's flank', turning to me he said, 'Mr. Brickhill do go to Col. Pulleine and ask him to send us help, as they are outflanking us here on the right.'

He went away towards the stony Kopje, followed by several of the soldiers. I went round the Volunteer Camp to that of the 2/24th. I saw several men but no Officer. I saw one of the guns brought to the corner of the Camp. The men jumped off and took to their heels.

There was no Officer to guide, no shelter to fall back upon.

The Basutos had a narrow escape of being cut off at the crest, but came through past the General's Camp. They shouted to one another and kept up the fire from a few rocks under Isandhlwana. The Zulus for the last 300 yds did not fire 25 shots, but came on with a determination of walking down the Camp by force of numbers. I consider that there were 30 to 1 of us. At 150 yds they shouted 'Usutu', and came on with an overwhelming rush. I went back to the 1/24th Regt. Camp to see if I could find the Quartermaster but could not, and seeing that the Zulus were already stabbing in this Camp as well as in the others I joined the fugitives retreating over the nek, on reaching which I found that all communication by the road we had come along was cut off by several lines of Zulus running across. These were evidently those Zulus who had been compelled to go over the nek by the fire of the Basutos. They had come along behind Isandhlwana and thus intercepted our retreat. The Zulus left horn had now come over the ridge South of stony Kopje. They could have completed their circle but I think preferred leaving this gap so that they might attack us in our flight, to bringing us to bay, when each man would have done his best.

The Isandhlwana horn edged us away more and more to the left and these two kept up a constant crossfire upon us. Our flight I shall never forget. No path, no track, boulders everywhere, on we were borne now into some dry torrent bed, now weaving our way amongst trees of stunted growth, so that unless you made the best use of your eyes you were in constant danger of colliding against some trees or finding yourself unhorsed at the bottom of some ravine. Our way was already strewn with shields, assegais or spears, blankets, hats, clothing of all descriptions, guns, ammunition, belts, saddles (which horses had managed to kick off) revolvers, and I do not know what whilst our stampede was composed of mules with and without packsaddles, oxen, horses in all stages of equipment, and flying men. Man and beast apparently all impressed with the danger which surrounded us. One riderless horse, which ran up alongside of me, I caught and gave over to a soldier who was struggling along on feet but he had scarcely remounted before he was knocked off by a Zulu bullet. I came up with Band Sergeant Gamble 1/24th Regt. tottering and tumbling about among the stones he said, 'For God's sake give us a lift,' I said 'My dear fellow it is a case of life or death with me,' closing my eyes I put spurs to my horse and bounded ahead, that was the last I saw of him.

The next soldier I came up with said, 'Well I'm pumped, I'm done the Zulus can just come and stab me if they like.' He sat down quietly on a stone to await his death. A little further on I heard a sharp Wangani (what are you doing) immediately behind me, turning my head quickly I saw a well built young Zulu not more than 15 years old (I knew not before that there were any so young in the Zulu Army) his assegais still poised against me not 3 yds off, but his eyes turned towards a Natal Zulu who walked just behind my horse's heels. The upraised spear of the latter made the young Zulu quail and retire to a more respectful distance. I have not seen my unknown protector since. Whilst going down into a deep Donga, I saw Lt. Melville and Coghill and Conductor Foley about 200 yds ahead and to the right. A stream of Zulus running on this right was fast pressing them down towards the course we were on. After we had crossed this we were brought to a halt by a chasm which opened to view just in front of the horses, we were at this time under a cross fire but had to go back and follow the course of the Donga. The constant whir of the bullets made my ears tingle, and a mounted Infantryman impatient at our Indian file style of proceeding put his horse at the gully. The horse jumped far short of the mark and the rider lay crushed beneath it 12 feet below. We afterwards found a way across but it was very steep. A little further on I met Mr. Melville carrying the colour.

We proceeded some way when Mr. M. said, 'Have you seen anything of my sword back there?' I replied that I had not. Two of Durnford's Horse who were a little in front of us stopped now and then and fired at the enemy and then rode on again. Going down to the river we had some very bad country, so bad that we all dismounted and led. Here we were compelled to take a narrow pass, and there was a great crush.

I kept my horse back to enable Mr. M. to get down as it was a very dangerous place if there had been a cannon. Mr. Coghill was just behind me and said, 'Get on your horse Mr. Brickhill this is no time to be leading a horse, get on with your horses you fellows in front there,' someone said, 'Get off yours this is no place to be riding.' I did not then know that he suffered from an injured knee and could not walk. As we got down to the bed we had to slide down a bank 8 or 9 feet high, Mr. Melville shot under a large tree and was nearly unhorsed by a branch which caught him on the right shoulder. I received the backward sweep of this branch on my left shoulder which tore my coat nearly off. The enemy were still in hot pursuit and we had a bit of bog to cross, this scattered us.

My horse got bogged and I lost my spectacles but a bullet close to me prevented my looking for them. The Buffalo was very high but there was no time to choose a crossing. The Zulus were making for a crossing higher up. I plunged in, my horse being at once off his legs, but had not gone 6 yards when he stumbled over a boulder and nearly fell forward, I seized his mane and guided him carefully and yet 4 times I thought all was lost. A waterfall was just below us in which three riderless horses were struggling. Mr. Melville crossed safely but his horse could not climb the opposite bank. My impulse was to go to his assistance but his horse gave a plunge and I thought seemed to be climbing out. Coming up the hill this side of the river we were again under heavy fire. I saw one white man and one native shot here. Then I made my way to the Msinga Mission Station.

Burial of the dead

L T. Col. Black 2/24th Regt, wires from Rorke's Drift. Have just returned from second days work at Isandhlwana. Have not returns in yet but consider that over 300 bodies have been interred today. June 24th 1879.

24th Regt. Maj. Logan, 1st Battalion is about to retire, is en route to England from the Cape to arrange preliminaries.

The Capt. 'Watchman' of November 13th says 'By train on Friday next the Headquarters of the 1st Btn. 24th Regt. will leave this Garrison for Natal, embarking at East London on board the troopship *Tyne*, and in bidding the Corps farewell we desire to testify to the general good conduct of the men during the period of their being stationed at King William's Town. We could have wished that on this account the Regiment might have been allowed to complete its term of service in South Africa in this Garrison.

The 1st Battalion has been called upon to render a variety of service since it joined the Command in January 1875. In May of that year a Detachment of 300 men, under Maj. Degacher, now Commanding the 2nd Btn., was ordered to proceed to Griqualand West to uphold her Majesty's authority in that Province. Proceeding by train as far as Wellington the Detachment had to make a long and tedious march, which was successfully accomplished, and remained on the diamond fields until November when it rejoined Headquarters at Cape Town, returning by an equally tedious overland route. In December of the same year a Detachment joined this Garrison but was subsequently called to Cape Town. In August 1876, a detachment was sent to St. Helena, and served there up to the August following, when it rejoined Headquarters.

A party of 48 NCOs and men have been doing duty in the Transvaal as Mounted Infantry since April 1877, and in June of that year a detachment was sent from Headquarters to Natal, but rejoined the Regt. on its coming to the Eastern Frontier in August. The 1st Btn. proceeded to the Transkei on the return of Kreli's people in force into Galekaland after their having been driven across the Bashee by a body of hastily raised Colonial Troops and Fingo Levies. Col. Glyn Commanding the Regt. was then placed in Command of the Troops serving against the enemy across the Kai, and his men participated in all actions against the Galekas. The Regimental Band also manned a couple of guns in the operations against the rebels in the Perie and their services as Artillerymen were highly commended by the Commander in Chief. During its period of service in Galekaland the Corps constructed and occupied Ports at Malans Mission, Beecham Wood, and Indutwa. In the operations in the Waterkloof and Shelmkloof one Company took part, and then marched to Galekaland. Half of the Battalion occupied this garrison till June last, and the remainder was drawn from the Transki and came into Barracks in August. Since then a Company has been detailed for service at St. Johns River, our latest acquisition of Territory, and, later still, two Companies under Lt. Col. Pulleine were sent to strengthen the Garrison in Natal and now the Headquarters are to go to the same station. This record shows how much travelling about the Corps has had in the course of four years that it has been in the Command, and the special services rendered by Officers and men taken from its strength must add to its reputation. We have already referred to the Mounted Infantry and to the Artillerymen it supplied, but we have yet to mention the raising of a body of 'Rangers' by Lt. Col. Pulleine and that of the Frontier Light Horse by Capt. Carrington. The latter

Corps is still in existence, and has done, and is still doing excellent service. And now, in parting with the Regt. we have much pleasure in stating that it leaves the Garrison without a blemish and that it leaves a reputation for having rendered valuable service to the Colony. Its Commanding Officer Col. Glyn, won the respect of those with whom he was thrown into contact whilst discharging a Military Command over mixed Imperial and Colonial Troops.

End Notes

1. Robinson, Chas, N., *Celebrities of the Army* (London: George Newnes, Limited, 1900)

2. G. Paton, Farquhar Glennie, William Penn Symons (authors/editors) *Historical Records of the 24th Regiment from its Formation in 1689* (1892)

3. Burnett, Maj. C. K., *The 18th Hussars in South Africa: The Records of a Cavalry regiment during the Boer War, 1899–1902* (Winchester: Warren & Son, 1905)

4. Symons was promoted to Major-General (Local Lieutenant-General) 'For distinguished service in the field', *London Gazette* 28 October 1899. He also received the Order of Bath (KCB) for his conduct during the Waziristan Expedition and was Mentioned in Despatches on four occasions. Note: See Holmes N., *The Noble 24th* (London: Savannah, 1999) for extensive detail on Symons' military service.